AR PTS: 1.0

Life in the Old West

BANDANNAS, CHAPS, AND TEN-GALLON HATS

Bobbie Kalman

🌱 Crabtree Publishing Company

LIFE IN THE OLD WEST

Created by Bobbie Kalman

To Betty Andres
who keeps my life wrinkle-free

Author and Editor-in-Chief
Bobbie Kalman

Managing editor
Lynda Hale

Senior editor
April Fast

Project editor
Heather Levigne

Researcher
Sarah Dann

Copy editors
Kate Calder
Hannelore Sotzek

Special thanks to
Pioneer Arizona Living History Museum; Jerri Stone,
National Cowboy Hall of Fame; Jim Bowman,
Glenbow Archives; Montana Historical Society

Computer design
Lynda Hale
Robert MacGregor (cover concept)
Campbell Creative Services

Production coordinator
Hannelore Sotzek

Separations and film
Dot 'n Line Image Inc.

Printer
Worzalla Publishing Company

Crabtree Publishing Company

350 Fifth Avenue
Suite 3308
New York
N.Y. 10118

360 York Road, RR 4
Niagara-on-the-Lake
Ontario, Canada
L0S 1J0

73 Lime Walk
Headington
Oxford OX3 7AD
United Kingdom

Cataloging in Publication Data
Kalman, Bobbie
  Bandannas, chaps, and ten-gallon hats

(Life in the Old West)
Includes index.
ISBN 0-7787-0073-9 (library bound) ISBN 0-7787-0105-0 (pbk.)
This book describes the various articles of clothing worn
by cowboys and others who lived in western North America
during the nineteenth century.

1. Costume—West (North America)—History—19th century—
Juvenile literature. 2. Cowboys—West (North America)—
Costume—Juvenile literature. 3. Indians of North America—
West (North America)—Costume—Juvenile literature.
[1. Costume—West (North America)—History. 2. Cowboys—
Costume.] I. Title. II. Series: Kalman, Bobbie. Life in the Old West.

GT617.W47K35 1999   j391'.00978   LC 99-10311
                                                 CIP

TABLE OF CONTENTS

SHIRTS, VESTS, AND COATS

These men have washed, shaved, and put on their best clothes to have their picture taken. They are wearing suits with vests. They did not work in these clothes.

Cowboys wore long-sleeved shirts made of wool, flannel, or cotton. Some shirts had collars, and others were collarless. A few were striped or checked, but most were plain. Cowboys never wore red shirts because they believed that the bright color would startle the cattle and cause a stampede. We now know that cattle cannot see red.

Warm and dry

A coat protected a cowboy's body from sharp thorns and wet weather. Most cowboys, however, found that coats were too tight and uncomfortable for working and wore them only when it was necessary.

Slippery slickers

Many cowboys wore a **slicker** to keep themselves dry and warm when it rained. These long canvas or leather coats were coated with grease so they would shed water. Cowboys often painted their coat to seal the fabric and make it windproof.

Winter wear

Some northern cowboys wore long overcoats lined with fur. Fur-lined overcoats provided extra warmth while working in snowy weather.

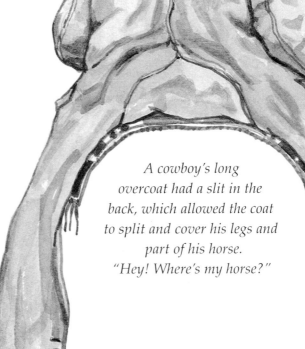

*A cowboy's long overcoat had a slit in the back, which allowed the coat to split and cover his legs and part of his horse.
"Hey! Where's my horse?"*

A good in-vest-ment

Cowboys could not carry personal items in their pant pockets. Reaching into pant pockets and handling a horse at the same time is difficult to do! Instead, cowboys wore a vest with pockets for carrying small objects such as a knife, a money pouch, and a pencil and notebook to keep track of cattle. Not only were vests useful, but they also kept cowboys warm in cold weather.

COWBOY HATS

Spanish sombrero

crown

brim

Mexican sombrero

Old-time Texas hat

A cowboy's hat was his crowning glory! It had a wide brim and high crown. Cowboy hats were made of brown, gray, or black wool felt. Some cowboys used a neck string to keep their hat from flying away in windy weather.

Hat tricks

A cowboy hat had many uses. It protected a cowboy's head and neck from sun, wind, and rain. It provided shade in the summer and warmth in the winter. Cowboys used their hat to carry water and food to their horses. Hats were also used to fan fires and swat flies.

Prized possessions

Cowboy hats were prized possessions! They were considered a symbol of strength and hard work. It was impolite for most men to wear a hat indoors, but a cowboy was never asked to remove his. In fact, cowboys rarely took off their hat, and some even slept with their hat over their face!

There were even superstitions about cowboy hats. When a cowboy undressed for bed, he never put his hat on top of his bed because he believed it was bad luck to do so!

Personal style

Each cowboy tried to make his hat a little different from those of others. Some cowboys bent the crown or brim into a particular shape. Others wrapped a band around the crown. Some bands were woven from horsehair or **rawhide**, whereas others were a solid strip of leather. Silver studs decorated the bands of some cowboy hats.

Durable Stetsons

Cowboy hats were handmade until a hatter named John B. Stetson opened a factory in the 1870s. Stetson produced a variety of cowboy hats known as **Stetsons**. Cowboys wore Stetsons because they were durable, waterproof, and held their shape well. The first Stetson was called the Boss of the Plains, a term that was used to describe cowboys.

Ten-gallon

In Spanish, the word gallon refers to a band on a hat. The more gallons on a hat, the more expensive it was. A hat with ten gallons was very impressive! Cowboys later used this term to describe a hat that was large and expensive.

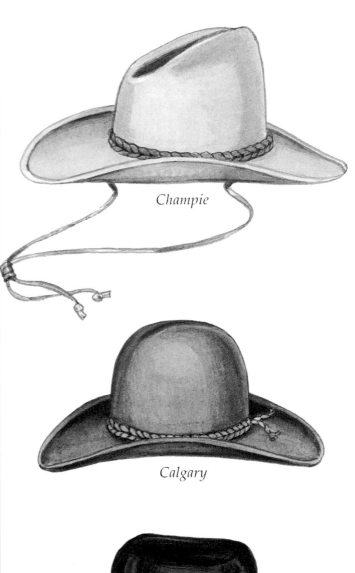

Champie

Calgary

Dakota

*This **bronco buster**, or horse tamer, is hanging on to his hat so he will not lose it. Sometimes a cowboy whacked a horse with his hat to help control the animal.*

BOOTS AND SPURS

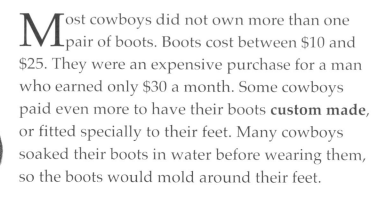

Most cowboys did not own more than one pair of boots. Boots cost between $10 and $25. They were an expensive purchase for a man who earned only $30 a month. Some cowboys paid even more to have their boots **custom made**, or fitted specially to their feet. Many cowboys soaked their boots in water before wearing them, so the boots would mold around their feet.

Proud as a peacock!

Cowboys took pride in their appearance and were very proud of their boots. They paid extra money for details such as decorative stitching, **inlaid designs**, and soft leather. Silver spurs completed the footwear, and their jingling sound drew attention as the cowboy strutted proudly around town!

I've got spurs...

Spurs were worn over boots. They were an extension of the cowboy's heels while he was riding. Spurs were usually made of silver and iron. They consisted of seven parts—a chap hook, rowel, shank, spur button, spur strap, heel band, and heel chains.

early cowboy boot

later cowboy boot

The early cowboys wore boots that were comfortable for walking but not suitable for riding horses. The rounded toe and flat heel did not grip the stirrup properly. Cowboys soon discovered that the boots worn by the vaqueros were better for riding horses. These boots were made of fine leather and had fancy stitching.

A spur for all occasions

Most cowboys had two sets of spurs. They used their work spurs every day and wore their fancy spurs on special occasions. Fancy spurs were engraved and often had **jinglebobs** on them. Jinglebobs were small pendants that dangled and made jingling noises when the cowboy walked. When he was riding, the jingling sound soothed his horse.

Mule ears are leather straps used to pull on tight boots.

Stitching makes the leather stiff and strong.

Spurs are used to urge a horse to speed up or slow down.

The vamp is the part of the boot that is crossed by the spur strap.

The toe of the boot is narrow to slide easily into and out of the stirrup.

The sole is made of thin leather so a rider can feel the stirrup and guide the horse properly.

A high heel prevents the boot from slipping out of the stirrup.

Spanish colonial spur

The chap hook holds the cowboy's pants and chaps away from the rowel.

The heel band helps hold the spur securely on the boot.

The rowel is the spiked wheel at the end of the shank.

The shank is the bar between the rowel and heel band.

jinglebobs

fancy spur

work spur

ALL-PURPOSE BANDANNAS

The first bandannas were plain white neckerchiefs. They were made from a square piece of cotton fabric that was folded into a triangle and tied around a cowboy's neck. In the late 1800s, clothing manufacturers dyed the fabric bright colors. These colorful neckerchiefs became known as bandannas. Bandanna comes from a Hindi word that refers to dyeing fabric.

Protection from heat and cold

Bandannas helped a cowboy in several ways. A bandanna kept the hot sun from burning the cowboy's neck. Sometimes cowboys bunched up their bandanna inside the crown of their hat to keep the heat of the sun away from their head. A bandanna soaked in water helped quench a cowboy's thirst during hot, dry weather.

First aid

The work done by cowhands was dangerous, and sometimes they were injured. There were few medical supplies to take care of wounds. A bandanna often doubled as a bandage to stop the flow of blood from a wound or the spread of poison from a rattlesnake bite.

In cold weather, many cowboys tied their bandanna over their hat to cover their ears.

This cowgirl is using her bandanna to bandage a cut.

Cowboys used their bandanna to filter out dirt from their drinking water.

When riding a horse or driving a wagon over dusty ground, cowboys pulled their bandanna over their nose to keep from breathing in the dirt kicked up by their horse.

USEFUL PIECES

A cowboy's equipment included his saddle, **lariat**, and **quirt**. Accessories such as gloves and cuffs not only looked good, they also helped a cowhand do his or her work more easily and safely.

The western saddle

When settlers arrived in the West, they brought with them saddles designed for horse racing and leisure riding. These saddles had a lightweight padded seat and a low **pommel**, or saddle horn. Cowboys used western saddles made of heavy leather and designed for long hours of riding and hard work. The western saddle had a high pommel and a raised **cantle**. The cantle is the rear part of the seat. A cowboy could wrap his lariat tightly around the pommel when roping cattle. The cantle held him securely in his seat when his horse made a sharp turn or abrupt stop.

quirt

Cowboys used a rope called a lariat to catch runaway cattle and horses. The word lariat comes from the Spanish words *la reata*, which mean "the rope." Lariats were as long as 60 feet (18 meters). Cowboys braided their own ropes from rawhide, horse hair, or **hemp**. A whip called a quirt was used for taming horses.

lariat

(opposite page) It was important for a cowboy to own a good, strong saddle because he sometimes spent fifteen hours a day sitting in it. A saddle was expensive, but it usually lasted many years. Cowboys looped their lariat over the saddle horn so the rope would be handy if they needed it.

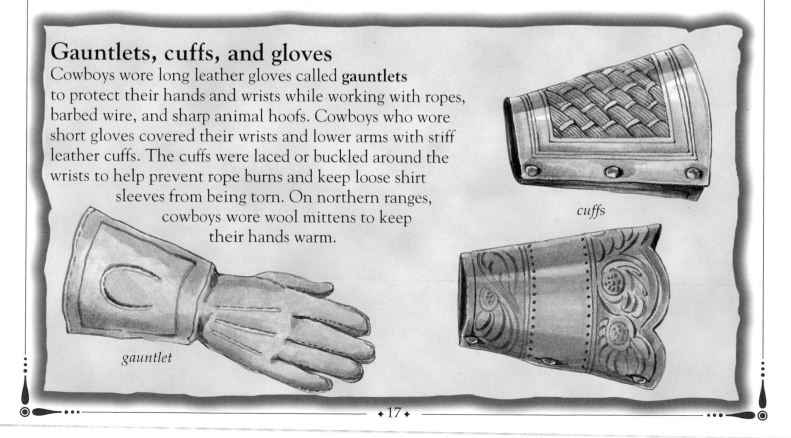

Gauntlets, cuffs, and gloves

Cowboys wore long leather gloves called **gauntlets** to protect their hands and wrists while working with ropes, barbed wire, and sharp animal hoofs. Cowboys who wore short gloves covered their wrists and lower arms with stiff leather cuffs. The cuffs were laced or buckled around the wrists to help prevent rope burns and keep loose shirt sleeves from being torn. On northern ranges, cowboys wore wool mittens to keep their hands warm.

cuffs

gauntlet

NATIVE AMERICAN CLOTHING

Before there were cowboys in the West, many Nations, or groups of Native Americans, lived there. Each Nation had a different culture, but most hunted buffalo. They ate buffalo meat, slept in buffalo-skin **tipis**, and made clothing from buffalo hides. The buffalo hunters were known as the Plains Nations. They used **buckskin** to make most of their clothing. Buckskin is animal hide that has been dried, stretched, and softened.

Men's clothing

Native American men wore fringed buckskin leggings held up by strips of leather that were attached to a belt. In cool weather, they wore a loose-fitting shirt, which was made of two buckskins joined with rawhide **thongs**. The hide from the animal's legs formed the sleeves.

These hunters are dressed for warm weather. Their lightweight clothes allow them to move quickly and easily.

Women's clothing

Women's clothes were also made from buckskin. Women wore a long, loose dress over their leggings, shown right. Dresses had a plain neck and were often worn with several necklaces. Most were also decorated with fringes.

Ceremonial clothing

Native Americans wore special clothing for ceremonies. Symbols were often painted on the buckskin with natural dyes. Clothing was decorated with quills, fringes, and colorful beads. Animal teeth, bones, fur, and claws were sewn onto the clothing or worn as necklaces.

(left) In winter, men and women wore buffalo robes made of softened hides with the animal's fur still attached. The fur was worn against the skin for warmth. Pictures telling stories of personal deeds were painted on the hides.

Moccasins were buckskin shoes. Each nation wore a unique style of moccasin. Some moccasins had a buckskin body and a separate sole of rawhide. Ceremonial moccasins were decorated with colored beads, porcupine quills, and fringes of skin or fur. Cold-weather moccasins were lined with fur.

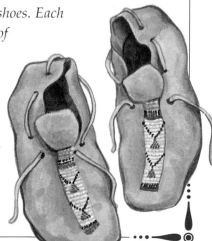

Sheared of its heavy winter wool, a sheep watches curiously as a woman spins the wool from its body into yarn. She will use the yarn to make pants, shirts, and long underwear for her family.

Many of the settlers had to make their own clothes and even wove their own cloth. **Homespun** was a fabric spun and woven from wool. Some settlers raised sheep for their wool. Others bought it from local ranchers or at a general store. Women **carded**, or combed, the sheared wool in order to untangle the curly fibers. They used a spinning wheel to spin the wool into yarn and then wove the **yarn** into fabric on a **loom**.

Other materials

Some people did not have spinning wheels or wool. The clothes they brought to the West were the only ones they had to wear. These settlers had to use any available materials they could find to make new clothing. Nothing was wasted! They cut up old tents and wagon covers to make overcoats and work clothes. Children's garments were often made from the worn-out clothing of parents.

Making buckskin

Some settlers made clothes from buckskin. They learned from the Native Americans how to soften animal hides such as deer and buffalo.

First, the settlers stretched the hide on a frame or on pegs hammered into the ground. They scraped off the fur and flesh until the hide was the same thickness all over. After scraping off the fur, they rubbed an oily mixture of brains, liver, ashes, and fat into the hide. They then soaked the hide in water to soften it.

The settlers stretched, pulled, and rubbed the softened hide with a bone or horn to make it smooth and then left it to dry. Once dried, the buckskin could be easily cut and sewn into pants, shirts, coats, and shoes.

This settler is wearing a buckskin shirt, pants, and shoes. Buckskin clothing was soft and comfortable.

READY-MADE CLOTH AND CLOTHES

In the early days, women made clothes for their entire family. If there was a general store nearby, they bought fabrics there. Families who could afford to pay a tailor or dressmaker had their clothing made for them. Some clothing could also be bought ready-made. Fabrics and ready-to-wear clothes were made in factories in the East. They were then shipped to the West by train and sold in general stores.

Tailors and dressmakers

As towns grew, many skilled people opened businesses. Dressmakers and tailors were in great demand by those who could afford to have clothes sewn for their family. As well as sewing clothes, dressmakers also sold items such as hats, gloves, and other accessories in their shop.

Making patterns

Dressmakers and tailors needed **patterns** to make new clothes. Old dresses and suits were often taken apart carefully, and their pieces were used as patterns. The woman in the photo, left, is cutting a pattern from paper. She can reuse the paper pattern many times to make new clothes.

Made by hand

Before sewing machines were invented, all ready-made clothing was sewn by hand. A finished garment took a long time to complete. Tailors used tools such as iron needles, shears, short knives, and **flatirons**. A flatiron is a heavy iron that is heated over a fire or on a stovetop and is used to press wrinkled fabric.

*(top) Women bought cotton fabrics such as **calico** from the general store to make clothing at home.*

From East to West

In the late nineteenth century, railroads were built to connect cities across North America. Settlers in the West were able to purchase many items, including clothing. These items were transported to the West by train. Before the railways were completed, clothing and other goods were hard to find in the West.

Mail-order catalogs

The railroad also allowed settlers to order goods from **mail-order companies** such as Sears-Roebuck and Montgomery Ward. These companies advertised their merchandise in catalogs. Before long, people began to order fashionable, ready-made clothing from catalogs instead of making all their clothes by hand.

(top) The invention of the sewing machine in 1851 allowed dressmakers to make good-quality clothes quickly. By the end of the nineteenth century, many new machines were developed to perform tedious tasks such as weaving fabric, cutting out patterns, and sewing buttons onto clothes.

(left) After many months of hard work, a cowboy's clothes were torn and ragged. When he had earned enough money, he replaced his worn-out clothing with new boots, pants, shirts, and vests. Cowboys bought the most durable clothing they could find because they did not want it to wear out quickly.

FASHIONABLE CLOTHING

People who wore fashionable clothing usually lived in town. Townspeople did not get their clothes dirty doing hard physical work. They worked in hotels, restaurants, and shops and wore fine clothes every day.

Men's fashions

Most men wore three-piece suits made up of pants, a vest, and a jacket. Suits were usually made of black or dark-brown wool. The vest buttoned up to the shirt collar. Men wore collarless cotton shirts and added a paper collar around their neck. Paper collars were thrown out when dirty. Collarless shirts did not have to be washed as often as those with collars because the rest of the shirt was covered with a vest.

Hats for townspeople

A man would not be seen in public without a hat. Besides cowboy hats, men who lived in town also wore **bowler** hats, which had a rounded crown and narrow brim. Hats were usually brown, black, or gray, but white hats came into style later in the nineteenth century.

Women's fashions

Fashionable women wore long dresses with a high neck and long sleeves. Their undergarments gave their dresses shape. Both the dresses and underclothes changed according to fashion. The skirts were wide enough to cover several **petticoats**, or underskirts. They were decorated with lace, ribbons, and bows. Some women wore a blouse and a long skirt.

(right) By the late nineteenth century, women were wearing more casual clothes, such as this suit with culottes.

(below) Although some could afford fashionable clothes, people in the West dressed mainly for comfort. Their clothes were less formal than those worn by women in the East.

COLORFUL CHARACTERS

Some of the famous characters who lived in the Old West are still remembered today. Many of them were known for their unique clothing. They wore unusual styles that reflected their strong personality.

Buffalo Bill Cody

William F. "Buffalo Bill" Cody was known for his Wild West Show, which toured North America and Europe for over thirty years. The show featured **reenactments** of famous battles and demonstrations of roping, riding, and **sharpshooting**. Buffalo Bill and the other actors dressed in cowboy costumes when they performed. In the photo shown left, Buffalo Bill is wearing fringed buckskin clothing. His costumes were based on those worn by real cowboys, but they were more flamboyant to add to the glamour of the Wild West Show.

Annie Oakley

Annie Oakley was the star of Buffalo Bill's Wild West show. She was an excellent sharpshooter and could perform tricks while standing on the back of a galloping horse. Annie's costumes were as sensational as her performance. In the late 1800s, most women wore long skirts and pinned up their hair in a bun. Annie wore short, knee-length dresses trimmed with embroidery and fringes. She wore a big cowboy hat decorated with a silver star and always wore her hair down. Annie called herself a "crack shot in petticoats." She won many medals, which she wore with pride.

(opposite) The performers in Buffalo Bill's Wild West Show were often real cowboys, but their clothes were fancier than those worn by working cowboys.

Glossary

accessories Extra items or pieces of equipment

bowler A man's hat with a round crown and narrow brim; also called a **derby**

branding The act of marking an animal's hide

bridle A harness used to control a horse

buckskin An animal hide that has been cleaned, dried, and stretched until it is soft

calico Brightly-colored cotton fabric

ceremonial Describing an object or act that is important or sacred

denim Heavy cotton fabric used to make jeans

gauntlets Thick leather gloves with long cuffs worn to protect the hands and wrists

general store A store that sells many different items in one large room

hemp A plant fiber used to make rope

Hindi The language spoken by the Hindu people of India

holster A leather case that hangs on a belt and holds a gun

homespun Plain, handmade, wool fabric

inlaid design A decoration that is set into a surface rather than raised above it

leggings Snug-fitting pants often worn under a long shirt or dress

loom A machine used to spin wool into yarn

mail-order company A business that produces goods, takes orders for them, and ships them to buyers through the mail

moccasin A soft leather shoe traditionally worn by Native Americans

patent A legal agreement allowing a person to sell a product he or she invented

pattern A design used to make clothing

pommel The horn on the front of a saddle

rawhide Animal skin that has not been made into leather

reenactment The act of recreating an historical event

rivets Copper studs used to make fabric stronger

sharpshooting The act of shooting a gun and hitting a difficult target accurately

thong A narrow strip of leather used to tie things

tipi A type of Native American home made of buffalo skins

waist overalls Denim work pants

Index

Acknowledgments

Photographs and reproductions:

Dean Cornwell, *The Cowboy Knitter*, National
    Cowboy Hall of Fame, Oklahoma City (detail):
    title page
Glenbow Archives, Calgary: pages 18 (bottom),
    20 (bottom), 24
Bobbie Kalman (taken at Pioneer Arizona Living
    History Museum): pages 5, 26, 27
Montana Historical Society, Helena: page 8
    Evelyn J. Cameron: page 21 (bottom)
    L. A. Huffman: pages 16, 21 (middle)
    Edward M. Reinig: page 21 (top right)

National Cowboy Hall of Fame, Oklahoma City:
    pages 7, 18 (top), 20 (top and right), 21 (top left),
    30 (top), 31
Other images by Image Club Graphics

Illustrations:

Barbara Bedell: pages 6, 7, 9, 10-11 (hats),
    17 (except lariat), 23 (right both), 26, 27,
    28-29 (bottom)
Antoinette "Cookie" Bortolon: page 29 (top both)
Bonna Rouse: back cover, pages 4, 12, 13, 14,
    17 (lariat), 25, 28 (top)

1 2 3 4 5 6 7 8 9 0 Printed in the U.S.A. 8 7 6 5 4 3 2 1 0 9